Acre (Akko) Travel Guide, Israel.

Tourism

Author
Carter White

Information-Source Publishing Notice

INFORMATION-SOURCE. This book is strictly prohibited from any illegal or unauthorized digital or physical reproduction including photocopying, illegal distribution, Electronic/digital manipulation, without the prior written permission of the publisher. Information-Source publishing holds anyone failing to comply with the above mentioned responsible, and will be pursued under Copyright law.

Copyright © 2021 Information-Source Publishing
All Rights Reserved.

First Printed: 2021.

Publisher:
INFORMATION-SOURCE
College House, 2nd Floor 17 King Edwards Road,
Ruislip London HA4 7AE.

Table of Content

ABOUT ACRE (AKKO) 9
- INTRODUCTION 9
- THE HISTORY 13
  - *Modern History*... 13
  - *Old History* 17
- TRAVEL GUIDE 25
  - *Guide to Acre* 31
  - *Culture: sights to visit* 37
  - *Attractions & nightlife* 43
  - *Shopping in Acre* 49
  - *Things to See in Akko* 55
    - Jezzar Pasha Mosque 63
    - Kibbutz Lohammei HaGetaot..67
    - Museum of Underground Prisoners 69
    - Subterranean Crusader City (Hospitalers' Fortress) 71
    - Rosh HaNikra Grottoes 73
    - Or Torah Synagogue 75
    - El-Jazzar Mosque 77
    - Fortifications..81
    - Ahmed Al-Jazzar Mosque 83
    - Citadel..84
    - Crusader City 85
    - Khan al-Umdan 86
    - Crusader Tunnel 87
    - St. John's Church..88
    - Akko Harbour...89
    - Hammam al-Pasha Museum..90
    - Old Town Souk...91
    - Bahje Baha'i Centre 92
    - Lohamei HaGetaot..93
    - How to Explore Things In Akko, Israel (Including A One-Day Itinerary 94
  - *Best Things to Do in Acre Akko [Israel Off the Beaten Path]* 109
  - *Top Restaurants in Akko, Israel* 124

Quick Guide for New Travelers.................................. 128
    Understand 129

About Acre (Akko)
Introduction

Akko's Old Walled City, a true architectural gem (and a UNESCO World Heritage Site), is in the process of becoming one of Israel's new overnight destinations. That may be because it's a natural base for touring the northwest quadrant of the country. But we're guessing that many find it difficult to leave Akko itself. With romantic minarets, authentic bazaars, adorable boutique hotels, unusual shops and eateries, an impressive ramparts, Akko (23km or 14 miles north of Haifa) has undeniable charm.

It also is loaded with history. Akko has been a port city for over 4,000 years. It flourished for centuries under the Phoenicians, Romans, and Byzantines and became the capital and last stronghold of the Crusader Kingdom before it finally fell in a.d. 1291. The Crusader city and fortifications lay in ruins until Akko was rebuilt in the late 1700s by the notorious Ottoman governor, El Jezzer (The Butcher) Pasha, who constructed a walled city filled with mosques, labyrinthine markets, travelers' inn, bathhouses, and mansions, all on top of the monumental structures of the forgotten Crusader city. Akko is divided into the New City, mainly built after 1948 and home to a mixed Israeli Arab and Jewish population, and the walled Old City, which is the main attraction inhabited mostly by Christian and Muslim Israelis.

Like many other cities in Israel, Acre (Akko) looks back on thousands of years of history. As a port city, Acre was the northern gate to Israel and therefore knew many wars and many different rulers. Two historical periods shaped the city more than others the Crusader Era and the Ottoman Empire.

In Acre there are more sights from the Crusader Era then in any other place in Israel, and for a good reason although the official name of the Crusaders' dominion was the Latin Kingdom of Jerusalem, for 100 of the 200 years that the Crusaders' state existed, Acre was the capital since the Crusaders lost Jerusalem to the Muslim sultan Saladin. After they lost Acre to the Mamluks, a Muslim dynasty from Egypt, the city was destroyed. Local governors in the Ottoman era rebuilt the city on top of the Crusaders' former city and so there are two cities on top of one another the Crusaders' underground ruins and the Ottoman-built city of today. The decisive moment for the Ottoman city came in 1799 when Napoleon put it under siege, but Acre eventually declined not because of a war but because of competition. At the end of the 19th century and the beginning of the 20th century, the port of Haifa was developed and grew to become the main port city in northern Israel. The port of Acre, whose importance had been second only to Jaffa, became irrelevant. But unlike the port in Haifa that cuts the city off from the sea, the Old City of Acre is still a residential district and a somewhat untidy and neglected tourist sight.

Acre is a half-day destination; at night there is not much to do in the Old City. With that said, there are a number of accommodation options.

The History

Modern History

Acre, Hebrew ʿAkko, Arabic ʿAkkā, city, northwest Israel. It lies along the Mediterranean Sea, at the north end of the Bay of Haifa (formerly Bay of Acre). Its natural harbour was a frequent target for Palestine's many invaders over the centuries. The earliest mention of Acre is in an Egyptian text dating from the 19th century BCE. The Bible (Judges 1) states that the city did not fall to the Jews under Joshua and his successors; the Canaanites and Phoenicians, Semitic peoples of Palestine and the Levant coast, long held the site. Later it was conquered by Alexander the Great (332 BCE) and by the Egyptian king Ptolemy II Philadelphus (reigned 285–246 BCE), who renamed the city Ptolemais.

Acre was a principal base of the Romans when they suppressed the Jewish revolt of 66–70 CE. Later conquerors include the Persians (614), the Arabs (638), and the Crusaders (1104), who named the city St. Jean d'Acre and made it their last capital. Its capture in 1291 by the Mamluk sultan al-Ashraf Khalil (reigned 1290–93) marked the end of Crusader rule in the Holy Land. From 1516 to 1918 Acre was, except for brief intervals, under the rule of the Ottoman Turks. In 1918 it was taken by British forces and subsequently became a part of Palestine under British mandate (1922).

The city's old fortifications and citadel were strengthened by Ahmad Pasha al-Jazzār (Arabic: "The Butcher"), the Turkish governor (1775–1804), and withstood Napoleon's siege (1799). Though the city had surrendered to the Egyptian viceroy Ibrahīm Pasha in 1832, the citadel itself had never been successfully forced until May 3, 1948, when, as a British prison, it was taken by the Irgun Zvai Leumi, a Jewish guerrilla group. Acre was occupied by regular Israeli troops on May 17, 1948. Though most of the city's Arab inhabitants fled during the Israeli takeover, about 3,000 remained; the city's population in the late 20th century was about three-fourths Jewish.

Acre's ancient port has silted up in modern times and has become secondary to Haifa's across the bay. It is used only by small fishing boats. Industries in modern Acre include a steel-rolling mill and match, tile, and plastic plants. Prominent structures, aside from the citadel, include the Great Mosque, built by Al-Jazzār and named for him; the Municipal Museum, housed in the Pasha's bathhouse; the Crypt of St. John, actually a Crusader refectory; and several churches built on Crusader foundations. Just north of the city is the tomb of Bahāʾ Allāh, Iranian founder of the Bahāʾī faith. To the south is a large industrial zone; paint factories are found in the east. The city remains the major trade centre for Arab settlements in western Galilee and is becoming popular with tourists. Acre is the site of the Nautical College of the Israeli navy. The city was designated a UNESCO World Heritage site in 2001. Pop. (2008) 46,100; (2019 est.) 49,380.

Old History

Akko (Acre) is a living city, which has existed continuously for about 4,000 years. Its beginning was in Tel Akko, more commonly known as Napoleon Hill. From the Hellenistic period onwards the city expanded west to the area that later became the Crusader and Ottoman city. The following historical review refers to the area known today as Old Akko and is based entirely on the "History of Akko" by Nathan Shore, unless noted otherwise.

Hellenistic Period
From the times of Alexander the Great (333-332 BCE) Akko enjoyed the same status as the Phoenician cities Tyre and Sidon, maintaining a direct connection with the Greek government. The use of coins was common in Akko and the local mint operated for about 700 years, until

the fourth century CE. Akko has the longest and richest numismatic history in Israel.

From 310 BCE, under Ptolemaic rule, Akko apparently received the status of Polis and was called "Ptolemais". The beaches of Akko appear in Greek sources of that period as a source for sand used in glass production. Akko reflects well the Hellenistic influence in Syria and Israel; as the largest coastal city in Israel at the time, Akko kept expanding in the peninsula area ideal for trading and gained strong political and economic status.

Roman Period
During the Roman period Akko's autonomous status as a Polis persisted. Many Jews settled in Akko in the beginning of this period and the city was connected to the history of the Jews in Israel throughout the Talmudic period. In the

early Christian period the Apostles Paul and Peter also stayed in Akko. During this period a long breakwater was built to create a safe harbor, which was Akko's main source of economic prosperity for about 1,000 years.

Byzantine period

Starting in the fourth century CE, the Byzantine period marks the strengthening of the Greek influence in Akko. The Tel settlement was abandoned and the economy continued to be based on sea trade. Following the great Jewish revolt of 614 Akko was the first coastal city to be captured. The Jewish community that flourished in Akko was apparently destroyed and the city remained abandoned.

Early Arab period (638-1104)

The beginning of the Arab period was marked by re-changing of the city name to Aka its original name in the Arabic form. The elite class in the city were mostly Christians. Yet a continuous process of conversion led to a reinforcement of the Islamic ruling class.

Following the rise of the Abbasid dynasty (750-1258) a cultural change took place which determined the dominance of Eastern values in Islamic culture. The Mosqes replaced the church, the statues in town squares were removed, while other cultural symbols prevailed.

Between the years 630 692 the city suffered from instability and fights with the Byzantines. In 660 the first Muslim shipyard was built by professional craftsmen from Persia, Beck, Homs and Antioch, who were brought to settle in Akko for this purpose. In 692 the Byzantines destroyed Akko along with Caesarea and Ashkelon. The seventh century

was a period of destruction after which Akko was restored only around the Old City area.

From 878 Israel was ruled by Ahmed Ibn Toulon who rebuilt and developed the port of Akko as a military base to strengthen his rule in Syria. In 969 the Shiite Fatimid dynasty, a naval power established in Akko, took over. There is evidence of Jewish presence in Akko during the twelfth century and by the end of the century Akko became a Jewish center.

Twelfth century (1104-1191)
During the Crusader period Akko was at its greatest and became one of the world's centers. Although its peak was a century later, in the twelfth century Akko was already the

largest and richest city in the Crusader kingdom as well as its most important port.

The city was conquered in 1104 by King Baldwin with a large fleet from Genoa in Italy. Despite the instability and hostility between Muslims and Christians the city enjoyed prosperity, security and cooperation between Europeans and locals. The city was inhabited by wealthy aristocrats and merchants leading luxurious lives and pilgrims crowded its streets. The city was subject to the king and ruled by his governor. Special rights were given to the merchants from Genoa who had their own quarter, as well as to traders from Venice, Pisa Amalfy and Marseille. Akko had the largest Italian Colony of any of the port cities in Israel and Syria. The substantial presence of Italian and French traders, who actually kept the connection between Europe and the Crusader Kingdom, established Akko as a crucial element of the East-West trade.

In 1187, following the Battle of Hattin, Akko was handed to Saladin without a fight. Most of

the Christian traders fled the city before the surrender. Apparently the city was severely damaged due to the resident's departure and the entry of the Muslim troops.

On the Third Crusade that came in response to the fall of Jerusalem and other cities, Akko found itself under the most famous siege in the history of the Crusades (1189 1191). The long siege, carried out by high ranking and religiously motivated participants, ended with the Muslims' withdrawal and the return of the Christians to Akko.

Thirteenth century (1191-1291)

The thirteenth century was the golden age of Akko as the capital of the Crusader Kingdom of Jerusalem. The city's population reached at least 40,000. Economically, socially and culturally Akko became one of the world's major cities. It was the most important trading center between Asia and Europe and the main Italian trade cities kept a permanent base in Akko. Most of the trade between the West and the Near and Far East passed through its port and markets. Akko was also a financial center of transactions and loans run by the Templars, and of real estate transactions in Europe led by the Hospitallers.

Crusader Akko was under constant threats from the Muslims and suffered from internal strife between its various quarters and communes. Any events taking place in the city had an effect beyond the country borders. In the eyes of the Christian West Akko symbolized the realization of the Crusader quest. There was a special cultural blending in Akko influenced by east and west. It was the home of the Kings of Jerusalem and other visiting rulers. It was the seat of the Supreme Court of the Kingdom which was the main

Travel Guide

Recognized by UNESCO as a World Heritage Site, visiting Acre (Akko) promises visitors an emotional journey to a glorious past and a one-of-a-kind experience. An ancient and wondrous city, Akko boasts many remarkable sites including the remnants of the Hellenistic-

Roman period as well as structures from the Crusader and Ottoman periods.

Much more than a historical and archeological marvel, Akko also has colorful Oriental markets, museums, beaches and water sports facilities, a fishermen's port, marina, restaurants, hotels, and annual picturesque festivals all that and more are just a few of the city's fantastic tourist attractions.

The city's fascinating historical heritage, its rare blend of East and West, authentic glimpses from the past and unique remnants from different cultures, have all made Akko into one of the most vital Ancient World cities.

The Knights' Halls
A magnificent tour of the halls of the Hospitallers Order's Fortress from the Crusader period. Discover the amazing remains of the

ancient Order, the renovated and stunningly reconstructed halls, courtyard and surrounding streets, and step into history as a 830-year old story unfolds before you within the halls of the citadel.

Be sure to visit the streets, chapels, stores and the Arts and Crafts Market, featuring artisans from the Crusades era, offering their wares: blacksmiths, glass blowers, potters, weavers, embroiderers, leather craftsmen, basket weavers, perfume and oil craftsmen, and more

Must sees in Acre
Not to be missed is the Hospitaller Fortress. There, you can wander through the enormous stone rooms with vaulted ceilings and perfect acoustics (try singing if you have a good voice!). The spectacular dining hall, dormitories and

even ancient latrine are in good shape and worth visiting.

In the large open courtyard, you can almost hear knights practicing their swordplay, loaded donkeys being led into the stables, and servants bustling back and forth from the well. The well is there, a keyhole-shaped structure now wisely covered by netting. A thriving caper bush grows inside. The well fills up twice daily, when the rising tide pushes the fresh-water source back upland.

If you want a feel for a real person who lived and died in the fortress, visit Peter's headstone on the way out. The Latin inscription and portrait of the knight etched onto the stone make you feel like you almost know this old Crusader.

At the end of the 12th century, the Templars built the Templar fortress, which was one of the strongest buildings in the city: they also built a 350-metre long tunnel, which leads from the fortress to the city port. It was only discovered in 1994 when some plumbing work was done in the area. The underground Templars Tunnel is great fun to walk through, as you hear the sea above and around you. If you're claustrophobic and a beanpole, this place might be tricky to navigate because it's dark and you have to bend over in some places.

The Turkish Bath House, one of the many layers of Acre history to walk through, is perfectly preserved. Colorful tiles walls enclose the space where all the important men came to steam their troubles away, while their wives held parties in a separate enclosure. There's also an entertaining movie that explains the history of the Bath House, inseparable from the history of Acre itself.

The Old City market is a great little place to check out some local produce at local prices. Watch out for some of the amazing Arab pastries in the bakeries. Your camera might work overtime here, with a plethora of sights and colors to capture. The market is perfectly safe by day, but a little more dodgy for strangers at night. Women should not walk alone there at any time. If it's an all-woman experience, come in a group of at least three. No need to be paranoid just smart.

Once you've walked through the market, head down to the Acre marina for some sea breezes and a wander past some of the old fishing boats. If you're feeling particularly touristy, be tempted by the hawkers selling you a ride on one of the tour boats. At ten shekels a person, it's a great little ride out into the deeper waters where you get a terrific view of the Old City walls.

Guide to Acre

Sightseeing in Acre what to see. Complete travel guide

A pleasant journey awaits you if you decide to visit the city of Acre (Akko) in Israel. This is a relatively small but, nevertheless, an interesting city. The hidden Israeli gem is situated in the northern part of the valley that shares the same name with the city. While taking a stroll in Acre, visitors will notice the width of local streets. They are quite narrow and still have their original look. Despite this fact, all buildings look spectacular regardless of their age. Tourists will find it interesting to visit colorful markets, the old port, and shops that sell fish. This is also the right place to relax at wonderful beaches of the Mediterranean Sea covered with soft sand. It is so pleasant to walk here or sunbathe under tender rays of Israeli sun.

The first settlement at the site of modern Acre appeared approximately in 3000 BC. Acre became one of the first cities conquered by Thutmose III during his military campaigns. When Alexander the Great conquered this territory, Greeks started settling in the region. At that time, there were no Jews in the ancient city. Only when Muslims managed to make Acre their own, the Jewish community started developing here. Later, the Crusaders claimed their authority over Acre, turning it into one of the leading trading centers. Starting from 1291, Muslims recaptured Acre thanks to the Mamluk invasion.

This was the most difficult period in the history of this region because the settlement was very poor. People lived in misery and could barely keep themselves alive. However, wars didn't stop in the territory of modern Israel. For centuries, the city continuously "changed" its rulers. In the end, Acre became a part of Israel, and the period of wars ended. This event took place in 1948.

There are several versions regarding the etymology of the city's name, but most of them sound more like a fairytale. One legend says that when the ocean was created it was expanding greatly until it reached Akko's walls. This is how the city got its name, which, in accordance with this version, means "up to here". Another legend mentions an herb with healing properties that grew here. This herb helped Hercules to cure his wounds.

The majority of Acre's population are Judaists, so traditions of this religion are dominant in the region. The most important tradition is to respect the Torah and Saturdays. On Friday evening, all shops close until Sunday. This rule doesn't apply to shops run by people of other religions. For example, Arab merchants can close their shops on Friday, and Christian shop owners usually have Sunday as their day off. However, there are not many shops of the latter two types.

The cuisine of the city of Acre in Israel is a combination of several cultures: Sephardic cuisine famous for its spicy and fragrant dishes, and Ashkenazi cuisine that is more popular with European nations. Jewish people prefer to eat kosher food. Having visited one of local kosher restaurants, you will not find food that contains pork and shell-fish. Needless to say that fans of other cuisines of the world Chinese, Arabian, Italian, French or Russian will surely find a charming restaurant or café to satisfy hunger.

Acre is a true treasure for tourists and guests of the city. The territory of Acre is like one big attraction. Everything here reminds of the old and rich history of this region. Families particularly enjoy taking a stroll on the streets of the city, looking at beautiful vases by Arab craftsmen, hookahs, and coffee brewing pots. Acre is incredibly rich in different items that look unusual for many European nations.

During a walk in the city's streets, tourists can reach the waterfront and enjoy a yacht ride for a moderate price.

As Acre is built along the Mediterranean Sea, local beaches are incredibly attractive and never stop luring new guests by their warm sand and hot rays of Israeli sun. Do you like walking on pebble, enjoying the massage-like effect? There is a pebble beach to the north of Acre. Local coastal water is clean and is suitable not only for adults but also for children. Argaman Beach and Palm Rimonim Hotel's Beach are among the most famous and popular beaches in the area.

Argaman Beach is paid for foreigners, but it has a well-developed infrastructure. At this beach, guests can use sun loungers, visit one of numerous restaurants, and rent different beach gear. Palm Rimonim Hotel's Beach is a part of the hotel complex. The beach is free for guests of the hotel. Everyone else needs to pay a fee to enter.

It is easy to reach Acre from another Israeli city, Haifa. Simply take the bus 251. It is also possible to arrive by train. A bus ride will be a bit longer, approximately 45 minutes, but this is a wonderful opportunity to see the suburbs and mesmerizing nature of the country. The train is faster and will take you to Acre in just 30 minutes. However, passengers need to stay alert and check all stops carefully in order not to miss the one they need because Acre is not the final destination.

Culture: sights to visit

Culture of Acre. Places to visit old town, temples, theaters, museums and palaces Citadel of Acre, which was built in the mid-18th century, is considered the main historic symbol of the city. This is a large architectural complex surrounded by impenetrable stone walls. Archaeological studies discovered that the first constructions on the site of the citadel were built by the Templars. The citadel that we can see today was built on the ruins. The underground part of the complex is the only surviving element of the older construction. Today, tourists can visit it too during an excursion in the citadel.

An ancient prison is one of the most interesting parts of the citadel. Hundreds of years ago, this was a prison for religious or political criminals. This part of the fortress still has its original look. Today, a thematic museum is open in the former prison. Visitors can explore the most secret parts of the citadel and see the military equipment that is still stored here. A walk on the fortress wall is one of the most exciting activities in the citadel because of the striking view of the coastline and the architectural complex.

There are several interesting museums in Acre-Akko. The Hamam El Basha Museum is recognized as the main cultural center in the city. A large part of the museum's exhibition is dedicated to the history of the ancient world. The venue exhibits a collection of ancient Roman sculptures, archaeological findings, and artifacts from different early periods. The historic museum is famous not only for its unique exhibits but also for halls with immersive illumination. Visitors have an opportunity to feel the atmosphere of an ancient city.

Al-Jazzar Mosque is the most outstanding religious landmark in the city. It was built in the second half of the 18th century by the order of Ahmad Pasha el-Jazzar. The mosque was built on the site of the destroyed church of the Templars. Starting from its opening, Al-Jazzar Mosque has been one of the biggest mosques in the country. The magnificent design in line with the historic traditions of the region deserves a separate mention. The mosque keeps a precious religious artifact a lock of hair of the Prophet Mohammad. The precious object is displayed on important holidays only. Muslims can enter the mosque but people practicing other religious can only admire its outer look. The tomb of Ahmad Pasha el-Jazzar is located inside the mosque, and this is another reason why the mosque is one of the most sacred places in the city.

The historic part of Acre-Akko is a unique architectural complex with the status of a UNESCO World Heritage Site. There are buildings of different periods and styles here. Unique and old buildings are everywhere. Old caravanserai buildings are particularly interesting for tourists. Khan el-Umdan is a true landmark of Acre. The luxurious caravanserai was built for wealthy merchants. It still has a charming inner yard and a warehouse section. Khan El-Farani is considered the oldest caravanserai in the city. It was initially built for French merchants. Today, the inner yard is the only part of the caravanserai that is open for tourists.

Do you like unusual excursions? How about visiting the underground city of the Templar knights? Archaeologists discovered this city relatively not long ago. The first underground streets and chambers were unearthed in the 50s of the previous century. Excavations haven't stopped to this day, and archaeologists keep discovering new and new halls and constructions. The underground city of Templars is located below the citadel. In the past, it was a part of the Templars' fortress. The underground part was used as a warehouse and a place to keep the stock of water. There were secret tunnels to different parts of the city and private rooms. A large part of these underground buildings is today open for tourists.

The Monastery of St. John Hospitaller is an interesting historic landmark. This is a large architectural complex with spacious halls that were once used to host important ceremonies and meetings of the royals. There is a secret tunnel made by Templars in the territory of the monastery. This tunnel is also an important historic landmark. Scientists think that the first tunnel here was built by Persians. Later, Templars significantly expanded and enlarged it. The length of the tunnel is 350 meters today. It starts near the north protective wall and stretches until the port area.

Attractions & nightlife

City break in Acre. Active leisure ideas for Acre attractions, recreation and nightlife

Besides walking in the historic quarter, Acre-Akko has prepared many interesting activities for its guests. Do not miss an opportunity to walk on the fortress wall that surrounds the historic part of the city. This wall is a fantastic observation area with striking views of the city and roofs of historical buildings. Local children use the old wall as a tower to swim into the sea. Do not follow them because this activity is quite dangerous. There is a popular restaurant specializing in regional cuisine right on the wall. The open terrace of the establishment offers a fantastic view of the sea. The panorama is particularly attractive at sunset.

Citadel's garden is a popular park located close to the citadel's entrance. This is a fantastic place to relax on a hot day. The garden is not big but it has a wonderful landscaped design and diverse flora. Visitors can see giant trees and slender palm trees, and attractive fountains provide refreshing coolness on hot days. Big trees make almost the entire territory of the garden shadowy, so this is a great place to relax when the temperature is high.

The Bahai Gardens is considered the biggest and most beautiful park in Acre. The park hides an important landmark the tomb of Bahá'u'llah, the founder of the Baha'i religion. For many years, this religion was an important part of the local culture. The large park lies in the immediate outskirts of the city. This is a place with incredible landscaped design. Visitors can see colorful, artistically made flowerbeds, admire trees and decorative bushes. Some parts of the park have green lawns with colorful flowers that form interesting patterns. It is easy to spend several hours in this beautiful place. By the way, several historical buildings are also open to visitors.

There are several interesting natural landmarks in the Acre-Akko suburbs. For example, Saar Falls is a beautiful waterfall that always attracts many tourists. You will be able to admire it only if you visit Acre at any time of the year except the middle of summer. The waterfall completely dries out in hot weather, so it is impossible to see it. Saar Falls is located in a beautiful mountain area. The seasonal waterfall got its name after the namesake river. There are many comfortable pedestrian bridges in this area that are also great as observation points. The beautiful area near the waterfall is also suitable for admiring rare plants. Many tourists prefer to visit Saar Falls in spring to see beautiful blooming flowers. By the way, it is better to explore this area together with a guide.

If you do not want to leave the city but still would like to admire beautiful nature, it is time to visit the botanical garden that is open in Acre-Akko. The garden is home to a large collection of plants brought from different parts of the world. Much attention is paid to the design of the garden, and that is why it always has interesting landscaped compositions.

Perhaps, Extreme Park is the most famous entertainment center in Acre. This is a large park with various extreme activities and amusements suitable not only for children but also for adults. The eye-catching design is not the only advantage of this park. The venue offers all kinds of amusements. There are a large, several meter high mountain climbing wall, bungee jumping towers, and Sky Track trails. Some amusements are available for adults and teenagers only, but small children will easily find exciting activities too. Once you feel tired, it is so pleasant to relax in a charming café that is open in the park.

There are several attractive bars in Acre, and it is great to visit them in the evening. Soul Burger is a stylish and modern venue. It offers a broad range of original drinks, signature snacks, and traditional Israeli cuisine dishes. Many people come to Soul Burger to eat its burgers with seafood, a signature dish of the bar. There is one more amazing thing about the venue it is open in a historic building with a perfectly preserved original design. Soul Burger's large halls are perfect for groups of guests.

How about relaxing in a casual setting and watching football? For this purpose, visit Exit, a popular bar that attracts local youth and sports fans. Besides a great choice of beer, cocktails, and signature snacks, the bar broadcasts the most popular sports events. On the days when there are no important football matches, the bar's staff connects game consoles to TVs and offers visitors to play and have fun with their friends.

Shopping in Acre

Shopping in Acre authentic goods, best outlets, malls and boutiques
The historic city center is the most interesting destination for shopping. There are many

artisan workshops in this part of Acre-Akko. The Old Town is also the location of the most interesting and colorful market in the city. This is the place where visitors can find the most popular local goods. Popular spices, sweets, and artworks made by local masters visitors can find all these and more. Besides them, there are charming restaurants and cafes. Gift sets with nuts and spices are the most popular souvenirs that tourists buy in the market. If you happen to visit this place, don't forget to try local baklava as it is so delicious. Handmade jewelry, accessories made from wood and glass are always very popular with tourists. Several shops that are open in the market sell shishas and all additional accessories for them.

Having explored the shopping streets of the historic district, head to local shopping centers.

Acre Mall is one of the most popular and largest malls in the city. There are a large food court area and a supermarket on the first floor of the shopping complex. The latter sells many popular locally sourced products. Both locals and tourists visit this supermarket to buy pickled olives and hummus, spices and fresh pastries. There is also a broad range of desserts for sale. Multiple clothes and shoe shops in Acre Mall usually offer moderately priced goods. There are several pavilions with sports clothes and shoes, backpacks and equipment for active recreation.

In Azrieli Akko, visitors will find shops by both Israeli and popular European brands. This is the best mall to visit when you need to buy attractive clothes, shoes, and accessories. Besides big stores, many small pavilions offer jewelry and cosmetics, accessories for smartphones and other gadgets, and souvenirs. Female tourists will find it interesting to visit local cosmetic shops. They sell high-class Israeli cosmetics with minerals and healing muds.

The historic White Market is a symbolic place for residents of Acre. Once it was one of the largest and most crowded markets in the region, but the importance of the White Market disappeared over the years. Nevertheless, there are still several dozens of vendors that offer their goods every day. All kinds of household items make up the majority of goods. It is also possible to buy inexpensive clothes made from natural fibers, colorful scarves, and shoes. Gastronomic pavilions at the market offer popular spices and sauces, halva, and attractive gift sets with sweets. The market is famous not only for a variety of goods that are sold here but also for its original historic architecture.

The most popular and interesting souvenir shops are located in the historic district of Acre-Akko. Pay your attention to David Miro Souvenirs. This shop offers a range of exclusive goods made by local craftsmen. Decorative copper plates with handmade embossing and drawings are among the most popular items sold in this shop. A big section of the souvenir shop is dedicated to jewelry. Besides them, visitors will find beautiful tableware, all kinds of souvenirs and amulets in Israeli style, ceramics, and other accessories. If you want to purchase inexpensive souvenirs, pay your attention to key chains and miniature plates. Are you searching for something special? In this case, you might like skillfully made figures of Crusaders and tiny copies of the most famous landmarks of Acre.

All sweet-tooths simply cannot fail to visit Nazareth Sweets shop that is located nearby. It sells dozens of different types of the most popular local sweets and desserts. Baklava and halva are sold by the weight and in beautifully decorated gift sets. If you haven't found what you were looking for, there is one more shop nearby that sells similar items Kashash. The shop has an adjacent café with the same name, so this is a great place to try all kinds of desserts and pastries, and buy the ones you liked in the shop afterward.

There are also several attractive supermarkets in the shop. Tourists who want to save on souvenirs should visit them in the first place.

May Market is a popular supermarket that sells not only fresh fruit and vegetables but also excellent quality canned food produced by local manufacturers. Female travelers will be excited to visit a cosmetic section with a choice of items and treatments based on the minerals from the Dead Sea. Finally, there is a section with sweets and wines, and the section with consumer goods always has a stock of toys and other accessories for children. Many foreign guests visit this supermarket to buy exotic fruits. When shopping in small shops and markets, don't forget to bargain before making a purchase. Bargaining is impossible in large shopping centers and supermarkets.

Things to See in Akko

Allow yourself at least a half-day to wander through Old Akko's medieval streets. Unlike the restored Old City of Jaffa, which is filled with tourist galleries, Old Akko is both charming and genuine, and its streets teem with real life. The best place to start your tour is at the Jezzar Pasha Mosque. Right across the street from Al-Jezzar Pasha's mosque is the marvelous Subterranean Crusader City, and just a few steps farther is the Municipal Museum (exhibits sometimes closed for renovations) housed in Ahmed al Jezzar Pasha's Turkish bath.

Next you'll wander through the pleasant and colorful streets of the bazaar. Be sure to see the most picturesque shop in the bazaar, Kurdy and Berit's Coffee and Spices, at no. 13/261 (ask around, it's deep in the market). The showcases here are filled with exotic objects and herbal remedies. If you make a purchase at Kurdy and Berit's, the very hospitable owner may invite you to try a cup of thick Arabic coffee. Also look for Abu Nassar's Oriental Sweets and Hummus Said, both located in the market near the Khan el Shwardia and each a legend throughout northern Israel. Akko's "formal" market is Suq El-Abiad, but numerous streets within Old Akko serve as shopping areas. You'll pass the El-Zeituneh Mosque

to the Khan El-Umdan caravansary, marked by a tall, segmented tower. A caravansary, or khan, was a combination travelers' inn, warehouse, banking center, stable, and factory traditionally built around a lightly fortified courtyard to house caravans, pilgrims, and other visitors.

At the port, you can hire a boat to take you on a sea tour of the city walls (about NIS 50 per person). Don't be afraid to bargain. Many boat operators will be glad to take you on a motoror fishing-boat cruise around Old Akko. Settle on a price in advance (about NIS 125 for an hour is average), and get a boat that looks comfortable.

In Venezia Square (Ha-Dayagim in Hebrew), facing the port, is the Sinian Pasha Mosque, and behind it the Khan El-Faranj caravansary. Yet another khan, named El-Shwarda, is a short distance to the northeast. A few steps back is the Jezzar Pasha Mosque. You'll also want to visit the dreaded Al-Jezzar Wall, where barbaric punishments were meted out, and the outer wall of the Akko prison, scene of a massive prisoner escape in 1947 (during the British

Mandate) engineered by the Jewish underground and dramatized in the film "Exodus."

The Top Attractions
Al-Jezzar's Wall
To appreciate the elaborate system of defenses built by Ahmed al Jezzar Pasha to protect against Napoleon's fleet and forces, turn right as you come out of the Municipal Museum/Museum of Heroism onto Ha-Hagana Street and walk a few steps north. You'll see the double system of walls with a moat in between. Jutting into the sea is an Ottoman defensive tower called the Burj El-Kuraim. You're now standing at the northwestern corner of the walled city. Walk east (inland) along the walls, and you'll pass the citadel, the Burj El-Hazineh (Treasury Tower), and cross Weizmann Street to the Burj El-Komander, the

strongest point in the walls. The land wall system continues south from here all the way to the beach.

Bahji

To Baha'is, this shrine to their prophet Baha' Allah is the holiest place on earth. Baha'i followers believe that God is manifested to men and women through prophets such as Abraham, Moses, Jesus, and Muhammad, as well as the Bab (Baha' Allah's predecessor) and Baha' Allah himself. The Baha'i faith proclaims that all religions are one, that men and women are equal, that the world should be at peace, and that education should be universal. Baha'i followers are encouraged to live simply and to dedicate themselves to helping their fellow men and women. They look forward to a day when there will be a single world government and one world language.

The Baha'i faith grew out of the revelation of the Bab, a Persian Shiite Muslim teacher and mystic who flourished from 1844 to 1850, and was executed by the Persian shah for insurrection and radical teachings. In 1863, Mirza Husein Ali Nuri, one of the Bab's disciples, proclaimed himself Baha' Allah, the Promised One, whose coming had been foretold by the Bab. Baha' Allah was exiled by the Persian government in cooperation with the Ottoman leaders to Baghdad, Constantinople, Adrianople, and finally to Akko, where he arrived in August 1868. He and several of his followers were imprisoned for 2 1/2 years at the Akko Citadel. The authorities later put him under house arrest, and he was eventually brought to Bahji, where he remained until his death in 1892. He is buried here in a peaceful tomb surrounded by magnificent gardens. Baha'is are still persecuted, especially in Iran where the faith was born; the Shiite Muslims in authority today look upon them as blasphemers and heretics.

You can visit the shrine at Bahji (Delight), where Baha' Allah lived, died, and is buried, on Friday, Saturday, and Sunday only, from 9am to noon. The house's beautiful gardens are open to visitors every day, from 9am to 4pm. Catch a no. 271 bus heading north toward Nahariya, and make sure it stops at Bahji.

Going north from Akko, you'll see an impressive gilded gate on the right-hand side of the road after about 2km (1 1/4 mile). This gate is not open to the public. Go past it until you are almost 3km (about 1 3/4 miles) from Akko, and you'll see a sign, shamerat. Get off the bus, turn right here, and go another short distance to the visitors' gate. The Ottoman-Victorian house holds some memorabilia of Baha' Allah, and the lush gardens are a real treat.

Jezzar Pasha Mosque

Ahmed al Jezzar ("the Butcher") Pasha was the Ottoman-Turkish governor of Akko during the late 1700s and notorious for his habit of mutilating both those in his government and those he governed. According to legend, on Al-Jezzar Pasha's whim, faithful chamberlains and retainers were ordered to slay their own children as signs of loyalty to him, and the Pasha rewarded government officials and loyal subjects with amputations of hands, arms, eyes, and legs to test their willingness to submit to his desires. If this was how he treated his friends, you can imagine the fate of his enemies. When Napoleon invaded Egypt, the English joined the Ottomans in trying to drive him out. Al-Jezzar Pasha marshaled the defenses of Akko, and the city withstood Napoleon's assault in 1799. Napoleon's forces never recovered, and Napoleon's dream of conquering Egypt died outside the walls of Akko. The Pasha died in Akko in 1804, to everyone's relief.

Ahmed al Jezzar Pasha's contributions to Akko included building fountains, a covered market, a Turkish bath, and the harmonious mosque complex that bears his name. Begun in 1781, it's an excellent example of classic Ottoman-Turkish architecture and stands among the

Pasha's most ambitious projects. It also illustrates how the traditional mosque complex worked.

As you approach the mosque area, Al-Jezzar Street turns right off Weizmann Street. The mosque entrance is a few steps along Al-Jezzar Street on the left. Before you mount the stairs to the mosque courtyard, notice the ornate little building to the right of the stairs. It's a sabil, or cold-drinks stand, from which pure, refreshing drinking water, sometimes mixed with fruit syrups, was distributed—a part of the mosque complex's services. Note especially the fine tile fragments mounted above the little grilled windows just beneath the sabil's dome. Tile-making was an Ottoman specialty.

Up the stairs, you enter the mosque courtyard. Your ticket will enable you to explore the complex of Crusader buildings, including a church (now flooded and used as cisterns) over which the mosque was built. Just inside the entry is a marble disc bearing the tughra, or monogram, of the Ottoman sultan. It spells out the sultan's name, his father's name, and the legend "ever-victorious."

The arcaded courtyard around the mosque can be used for prayers during hot days of summer, as can the arcaded porch at the front of the mosque. The shadirvan, or ablutions fountain, opposite the mosque entry, is used for ritual cleansing five times a day before prayers. You must slip off your shoes before entering the mosque proper.

Inside you'll notice the mihrab, or prayer niche, indicating the direction of Mecca, toward which worshipers must face when they pray.

The galleries to the right and left of the entrance are reserved for women, the main area of the floor for men. The minbar, a sort of pulpit, is that separate structure with a curtained entry, stairs, and a little steeple. Around to the right are a mausoleum and a small graveyard that hold the tombs of Ahmed al Jezzar Pasha and his successor, Suleiman Pasha, and members of their families. The mosque is still used by Akko's Muslim population, so when it's in service for prayer, you must wait until the prayers are over to enter the mosque.

Kibbutz Lohammei HaGetaot

The Ghetto Defenders' Kibbutz, 3.2km (2 miles) north of Akko, was founded in 1949 by a small group of survivors of Jewish ghettos in Poland

and Lithuania. Initially scattered in towns and refugee camps throughout Israel, they felt they could best rebuild their lives among others who had similar tragic memories as former partisans and participants in ghetto uprisings. The kibbutz flourished, and today their children and grandchildren manage the schools, factories, and beautiful orchards of this very symbolic community.

The Ghetto Fighters' House at Kibbutz Lohammei HaGetaot, the Museum of the Holocaust and Resistance, and Yad La Yeled, the Memorial and Museum of Children, together form Israel's second-largest memorial and museum of the Holocaust after Yad VaShem in Jerusalem. This complex, with its own archives and study programs, documents Jewish life in communities throughout Europe before and during the Holocaust. The complex contains a museum of writings, diaries, and artwork from the ghettos and concentration camps, and these detailed, very personal exhibits vividly inform about the ghetto uprisings and the destruction of Jewish communities, including those in Holland, Saloniki, Vilna, and Hungary. Among the many models and installations is a replica of the Anne Frank House in Amsterdam. Especially moving are the paintings and drawings done by children. The museum is the center for an international education program designed to teach about the Holocaust, in the hope that such knowledge will help prevent such cruelties from being permitted in the future.

Museum of Underground Prisoners

The complex of buildings, in the Citadel of Akko, was used as a prison in Ottoman and British Mandate times. Part of the prison has been set aside in honor of the Jewish underground fighters imprisoned here by the British. With the help of Irgun forces, 251 prisoners staged a mass escape in May 1947. If you saw the movie "Exodus," that was the breakout featured in the film and this was the prison. The prison is also revered by Arab Israelis and by Palestinians, whose own national fighters were detained and, in many cases, executed here during the British Mandate.

Among the exhibits are the entrance to the escape tunnel and displays of materials showing the British repression of Zionist activity during the Mandate. Not all prisoners were lucky enough to escape, however. Eight Irgun fighters were hanged here in the 10 years before Israel's independence. You can visit the death chamber, called the Hanging Room, complete with noose.

Inmates here included Zeev Jabotinsky and Dov Gruner, among other leaders of Israel's independence movement. Before the Mandate, the prison's most famous inmate was Baha' Allah (1817–92), founder of the Baha'i faith.

Subterranean Crusader City (Hospitalers' Fortress)

Virtually across the street from the Mosque of Ahmed al Jezzar Pasha is this Subterranean Crusader City, the town's unmissable site. In the entrance is a tourism information kiosk, where you can buy a city map and an entrance ticket.

The Crusaders built their fortified city atop what was left of the Roman city. The Ottomans, and especially Ahmed al Jezzar Pasha, built their city on top of the largely intact buildings of the Crusaders. In Ottoman times, the cavernous chambers here were used as a caravansary until Napoleon's attack. In preparation for the defense of his city, Al-Jezzar Pasha ordered the walls heightened, and the Crusader rooms partially filled with sand and dirt, to better support the walls. Today, you get a good look at how the Crusaders lived and worked in the late 1100s, from the ruined Gothic church to the dungeons and massive gathering halls. A highlight is the Knights' Halls, once occupied by the Knights Hospitalers of

Saint John. In the ceiling of the hall, a patch of concrete marks the spot where Jewish underground members, imprisoned by the British in the citadel (directly above the hall), attempted to break out. Be sure to pick up a headset at the entrance so you understand the significance of what you're seeing.

Rosh HaNikra Grottoes

The bluer than blue waters in these natural Israeli caves are reached via the world's steepest cable car.

Located On The Coast Near the border to Lebanon, Israel's Rosh HaNikra Grottoes are a popular nature site that was once only available to divers, but thanks to the installation of the world's steepest cable car, anyone can come and see the incredibly blue waters of these natural caves.

Through millennia of strong waves bashing up against the soft chalk cliffs on the Mediterranean Sea, large sea caves have formed around the base. Since their modern discovery these lovely geological anomalies have generally been open only to those with the skill and equipment to approach the formations from sea. However as the popularity of the site grew, a new solution needed to be devised in order to cater to the growing number of visitors clamoring to check out the grottoes.

To meet the rising demand, a cable car was installed to ferry tourists down to the site to check out the sea caves. The gondola cars carry from the top of the white cliffs to the bottom, covering over 200 feet in about two minutes. The speed of the ride is achieved by the stark slope of the cable lines which make it the steepest cable car system in the world. Were the cables any more vertical, the system would be an elevator.

Given the site's proximity to the Israel-Lebanon border also saw the creation of a famous train tunnel that can also be visited. However the bright blue waters filling the Rosh HaNikra Grottoes make that feat of human engineering seem a bit less impressive.

Or Torah Synagogue

This synagogue is covered in beautiful mosaics that explore the history of the Jewish people.
Just Outside of Acre's Old Walled city, lies the Or Torah Synagogue, also known as the Tunisian Synagogue in Acre.

The synagogue was first constructed in 1955 in line with a wave of Tunisian immigrants arriving in Israel during the 1950s and 1960s. The synagogue is widely credited with seeking to re-establish the Jewish pride seen in mosaics of ruined ancient synagogues found throughout Israel.

For over 54 years, the four floors of the synagogue were covered wall-to-wall in mosaic tiling crafted entirely on natural stones from all over Israel. The mosaics display Jewish history from the biblical age to the present day. Some designs display the enslavement of Jewish people in Egypt, others detail Jewish resistance during World War II. They also display various celebrations that take place during Jewish holidays.

The synagogue has silver doors that protect another set of doors to its main ark. There are seven Torah arks inside the synagogue. The doors themselves speak to the fight for statehood, they also pay homage to Jewish communities annihilated by the Nazis and their collaborators.

Stained-glass windows celebrate the state of Israel, depicting the Knesset and the Israeli flag. Today, the synagogue serves a large community of Sephardic Jews in Akko.

Know Before You Go
Visits to the synagogue generally need to be scheduled by calling in advance. The community is quite welcoming to people interested in the synagogue. It's appropriate to dress modestly when visiting.

El-Jazzar Mosque

A stunning mosque owes its design to an Ottoman ruler nicknamed "the Butcher."

In The 4,000-Year-Old Seaside City of Acre, the green tip of a minaret stands sentinel above two large domes of the same color, puncturing the otherwise seamless blue Mediterranean sky. Underneath the structure's spacious, palm tree-lined courtyard are a series of cisterns fed by water from the nearby Kabri springs. Also known as the Great Mosque and the White Mosque, this place of worship owes both its design and existence to a famous Ottoman ruler of obscure origins.

Sometime between 1720 and 1739, a young boy now known as Ahmed was born in what is today southern Bosnia. After moving to Constantinople, Ahmed worked for a period in Anatolia, eventually landing in Egypt, where he quickly curried favor with Mamluk officials. Mamluks were young Balkan (including

Bosnian), Circassian, Coptic, Turkic, and Georgian men who had been sold into slavery and trained as soldiers for their captors. At one point, these slaves revolted and took control from their former owners, although they kept the slavery apparatus running so as to have a continuous supply of future rulers and administrators.

After working his way up the Mamluk ladder of influence and power, Ahmed began leading military campaigns. Eventually allying himself with the Ottomans, Ahmed was entrusted with commanding soldiers in Lebanon. Having demonstrated his military brilliance, he was sent in the mid-1770s to defeat a prominent Bedouin named Dahir al-Umar al-Zaydani at Sidon, thus earning the position of governor.

He subsequently made Acre his capital and set about renovating it.

The Pasha's rule is characterized by a series of contradictions. He commissioned numerous architectural projects that are in large part responsible for transforming a pile of Crusader ruins into the city that Acre it is today, but he did so by imposing crushing taxes on the locals. While he successfully defended Acre from Napoleon's army, he was nicknamed 'The Butcher' for being excessively cruel to his enemies, be they the French or Bedouins.

Though there are rumors that Jazzar Pasha got his bloody nickname from cutting off the noses, ears, and eyes of Napoleon's soldiers, this is hard to verify, and may very well be a tale concocted by an embarrassed and defeated France. Others say that the title comes from his indiscriminate butchering of Bedouin raiders. Whatever the origins, it's safe to say that the better elements of The Butcher's complex legacy can be seen throughout the city, especially in the lovely green mosque, replete with a lush garden and marble and granite inlays.

Know Before You Go
Remember to wear clothing that covers your shoulders and reaches your ankles. There is a very small entry fee, so bring a few NIS with you.

Fortifications

Akko's incredible surviving walls, which wrap around the old city, are the town's most distinctive feature. For panoramic skyline views across Akko, walking along these ancient defensive barriers can't be beaten.

The fortifications were given their present form by Ahmed el-Jazzar in the 18th century.

From Weizmann Street, you can climb up onto the ramparts and walk to the northeast corner, dominated by the massive tower known as the Burj el-Kummander. It stands on the foundations of the "Accursed Tower," from which Richard the Lionheart hauled down the Duke of Austria's banner in 1191.

A little further south from here, sited in the walls, is the Treasures in the Wall Museum, which has an ethnographic collection of artifacts from early Zionist settlers in the area.

If you head back east along the wall, towards the sea, you come to the Burg Kurajim (Tower of the Vine). This Ottoman bulwark, built to defend the town against sea attacks, is built on

foundations dating from the Crusader period.
Address: Weizmann Street, Akko

Ahmed Al-Jazzar Mosque

Occupying the site of the Crusader cathedral, the Ahmed Al-Jazzar Mosque was built in 1781 on the model of an Ottoman domed mosque.

The courtyard is entered by a flight of steps, on the right of which is a small Rococo-style kiosk.

Surrounding the arcaded courtyard are rooms, which once provided accommodation for pilgrims and Islamic scholars. On the east side of the arcaded gallery, steps lead down to a cistern dating from the Crusader era, which provided a water supply for Akko's population when the town was under siege.

A small, plain domed building to the right of the prayer hall entrance contains the mausoleum of Ahmed Al-Jazzar, who died in 1804, and of his successor, Suleiman Pasha.

The mosque itself, with its tall slender minaret, is a fine example of Turkish Rococo architecture, with a mammoth interior decorated in ornate blue, brown, and white.

Address: Al-Jazzar Street, Akko

Citadel

The grand bulk of Ahmed Al-Jazzar's 18th-century citadel sits just inside the old city walls and is one of Akko's major points of interest.

The current Ottoman-era building is sited atop an earlier citadel structure that was built by the Crusaders.

During the British Mandate period, the citadel building was used as a prison by the British and today, houses the Museum of Underground Prisoners.

This museum commemorates the Jewish fighters who were imprisoned or executed here by the British authorities during the Mandate era, with a collection of black and white photographs and original documents from that time.

Address: Al-Jazzar Street, Akko

Crusader City

Underneath Ahmed Al-Jazzar's citadel is the highlight of a citadel visit. The Crusader City historic site comprises a fascinating series of gothic vaulted halls, which were once headquarters for the Knights Hospitaller.

There are six connected vaulted halls, as well as a dungeon to explore, with the Knights Hall and

Dining Hall the best examples of the grand, soaring Gothic architecture of the medieval Crusader period.

The non-claustrophobic can navigate their way through a narrow subterranean tunnel to the crypt after they've finished visiting the halls.

Khan al-Umdan

The Khan al-Umdan (Khan of the Columns) gained its name because of the granite and porphyry columns that Ahmed el-Jazzar brought from Caesarea to build this khan.

Built on the site of the Crusader's Dominican monastery, the khan provided traveling merchants with accommodation while trading in the city.

Set around a large rectangular courtyard, the ground floor rooms would have been used for storage and stables, while the upstairs would have been sleeping quarters for the merchants.

Over the north entrance is the clock tower commemorating Sultan Abdul Hamid's jubilee in 1906.

Address: Salah Bazri Street, Akko

Crusader Tunnel

If you're not claustrophobic, this eerie Crusader Tunnel is one of Akko's most intriguing tourist attractions.

It was discovered in 1994 by a local plumber. The subterranean passage would have originally connected the harbor with a Templar palace, providing a secret escape route to the sea in case of attack.

Today, it runs from HaHagana Street to the Khan al-Umdan and provides a fascinating glimpse into Crusader architecture.

A walk through here is highly recommended if you're at all interested in the medieval Crusader history of this town.

Address: HaHagana Street

St. John's Church

By far Akko's most picturesque church, St. John's Church was built in 1737 and occupies the site of an earlier 12th-century Crusader church dedicated to St. Andrew.

The church's interior is rather plain, and the main reason most people visit is to photograph the façade.

The juxtaposition of the church's crisp white walls and bright red bell tower surrounded by the crumbling stone walls of Akko's seafront makes this one of Akko's prettiest scenes for photographers. Come here in the late afternoon to capture the softest light.

Address: Salah Bazri Street, Akko

Akko Harbour

Now home to colorful local fishing boats and yachts, Akko harbor was a busy and important port from the classical age right until the medieval period.

During the Crusader era, it could sometimes be occupied by as many as eighty ships. The original port has now silted up, and all that is left is this small, tranquil fishing harbor.

From here, you can hop on a tourist boat to head out onto the Mediterranean and get excellent views of Akko Old City from the sea.

Hammam al-Pasha Museum

This old hammam (Turkish Bath) has been fully restored and is now home to an interesting museum with exhibits on the history and culture of the Turkish bath experience.

This hammam dates from the 18th century and is an excellent example of Ottoman-era bathhouse architecture and interior design. It was a working Turkish bath right up until the 1940s.

Visitors are walked through hammam history and traditional hammam practices with the aid of dioramas throughout the rooms, and an audio guide. The entire bathing process is explained along with the important place of hammam culture in day-to-day life.

Address: El-Jazzar Street, Akko

Old Town Souk

Akko's main souk (market place) is right in the center of the Old City and is a fun and vibrant bazaar full of fresh produce, cheap eats, buckets of spices, and souvenirs.

If you're looking for an original gift to bring home, it's a great place to browse for textiles and bric-a-brac, though you'll have to get your haggling hat on if you want a good price from the vendors.

If you're not shopping, strolling through this area is worthwhile simply to experience the bustle of local shoppers and take in the smells and sights of a traditional souk district.

Bahje Baha'i Centre

For some time out from historic sightseeing, take a trip to the beautiful gardens of Bahji, which contain the shrine of Bahá'u'lláh, founder of the Baha'i faith.

He was exiled to Akko in 1868 and spent the last years of his life in the red-roofed house in the gardens.

This is the sister site to the more famous Baha'i Gardens of Haifa. Although much smaller and more modest, Akko's garden is similarly immaculately manicured. It's also much less visited than Haifa's gardens, so it's very peaceful.

If you want to see the shrine, you have to join one of the organized tours that run in the mornings between 9am and noon. Otherwise, travelers are free to wander through sections of the gardens independently.

Location: 3 kilometers north of Akko

Lohamei HaGetaot

The kibbutz of Lohamei HaGetaot was founded in 1949 by Polish and Lithuanian Jews who had spent WWII fighting the Nazis.

It is home to a moving museum dedicated to the Jewish resistance and the Holocaust. On the ground floor are displays illustrating the history of Vilnius, the "Jerusalem of Lithuania," and the town's Jewish community from 1551 to 1940.

There is material on the early days of the socialist and Zionist movement at the end of the 19th century, and objects illustrating the everyday life of Polish Jews as well as an exhibit of some 2,000 drawings and paintings by concentration camp prisoners, including portraits of inmates

How to Explore Things In Akko, Israel (Including A One-Day Itinerary

Traveling to Israel and wondering whether Akko should be in your trip itinerary? We've been to Akko (aka Acre) many times and I can assure you it should be. Let me walk you through this amazing ancient city and show you all the fantastic things there are to see and do in Akko.

In this post, I'll tell you a bit about the history of Akko, and then walk you through the nine main attractions this city has to offer. By the time we'll finish the list, I promise you that you'll want to incorporate this unique travel destination in your itinerary.

So, What Is Akko Anyway?

Akko is a city along the shores of the Mediterranean, home to about 55,000 residents. This is one of the few cities in Israel with a mixed population of Arabs and Jews. According to the city's site (in Hebrew), 72% of the population is Jewish and 28% Arab. However, you'll be visiting the Old City of Akko where almost all of the residents are Arab.

The Old City of Akko is a UNESCO World Heritage site and for good reason: The city is over four thousand years old! Archeologists keep discovering more and more of the awesomeness of that history and you get to see it all when visiting.

Akko offers a thrilling mix of archeology, authentic Middle Eastern markets, the blue mediterranean sea, and some delicious ethnic food. It's a lot like the Old City of Jerusalem, only with a view to the sea. Let's start exploring what there is to do in Akko.

Is It Acre Or Akko?

In English, it's known as Acre. Why? As far as my research shows, no one really knows. I can tell you that the name in Hebrew is Akko and in Arabic Akka. Some suggest that Acre is some version derived from the Canaanite word Adco which apparently means "border", possibly because this area was the northern border of the Canaanite territory.

But that was literally millennia ago. These days, you'll still see the name "Acre" in travel books and in signs in the city itself, so the word is certainly in use. However, if you're traveling via public transportation and need to ask a local about your destination, you should really use "Akko" (or "Akka" if asking a native speaker of Arabic).

9 Awesome Things To Do In Akko, Israel

If you're looking to create an itinerary, let's kick off the list of things to do. Make sure you read through for more tips that will help you plan the best possible visit to Akko.

1. Walk Through The Halls Of The Knights

A thousand years ago the crusaders invaded the Holy Land to conquer Jerusalem back from the hands of "the Saracens" the term used at the time to describe the local muslim population. This was an age of romance and chivalry, when a knight in shining armour was a very real thing.

These knights built their own small town in Akko, complete with lively streets, thriving markets and a majestic fortress. They lived in Akko for a couple of centuries until the Saracens lead by Sallah A Din sent them back to Europe. Their cherished settlement was then covered in dirt and remained hidden from sight for centuries. It was only in 1990 that archeologists began to excavate the ancient town and bring it back to light. This ever-continuing extensive excavation and preservation project allows us to experience the amazing medieval town of the crusaders in a truly thrilling way.

Armed with an audio guide and a map, you are free to roam the excavated streets and alleys.

Sounds and colorful moving images bring the streets back to life all around you for a unique multimedia experience.

One of the tour highlights is seeing the great Dining Halls of the knights. You can actually have a wedding here these days, hence the huge tables and benches, medieval style. The original stone pillars and the colorful banners of the knights that surround you make it easy to imagine you've traveled back in time. Kids and grownups alike love these halls!

2. Visit The Medieval Market

Your visit to the Crusaders' Fortress will take you to a beautiful reconstructed market area where artisans engage in medieval crafts and arts. You can buy their art or just spend some time looking at them work. You are within the excavated city so the location couldn't be more perfect.

They even have game boards (rather than board games!) for the complete medieval market experience!

3. Follow The Underground Templar Tunnel

Indiana Jones meets the Da Vinci Code!

Have you heard about the secret order of the Templars? They too were here during the crusades and true to their secretive heritage they left their mark in the form of an underground tunnel connecting the fortress with the beach.

The tunnel was discovered in the 1990's and has since been fully excavated and made safe for visiting. There is sea water in the tunnel but fortunately they put in a wooden deck so you don't have to get your feet wet. You enter one end near the fortress and walk along the tunnel —Coming out to this view —

Which brings me to the next recommendation —

4. Breath In The Sea Air On The City Walls

Akko was a historic port city of strategic importance. During the 18th and 19th century, its Ottoman rulers fortified the city with a strong stone wall built around it. Today you can walk along the wall for amazing views of the Mediterranean. It's not always very clean but the breeze and views are worth it.

5. Taste The Local Food In The Market

Akko is famous for its Old City bazaar. It's absolutely worth a visit in its own right, so make sure to immerse yourself in the colors, sounds, and scents of this fishing port's market.

Sa'id's Hummus place is famous across the country and offers delicious fresh hummus with extras served with warm homemade pita bread. Yum! This is a popular lunch joint that can get crowded but that's part of the charm of this local experience. Don't be too late. Once they run out of hummus, they close for the day.

If you have a sweet tooth, you're in for a treat! Street vendors offer a variety of homemade authentic candy. These will preserve quite well so you can get a few pieces as gifts for your friends back home.

For a healthier option, try the variety of caramelized nut-based sweets. Every type of nut and seed is available, all baked in delicious caramel!

6. Visit The Hammam

The beautifully reconstructed Hammam is one of Akko's historic gems. Hammam means Turkish bath and this one was a center of local social life for centuries –

Yup, today the only ones enjoying a traditional back rub are these statues. The Hammam was turned into an interactive museum. A virtual guide takes you from one room to another telling you all about this establishment and the people who have operated it through the centuries.

7. Enjoy A Break Next To The Fountain

Need a break from all the walking? Looking for a place where you can sit down in the shade and nibble on the sweets you got at the market? Try the magical garden right by the visitors center (near the entrance to the Crusaders' Halls).

This is where your tour of Akko will likely begin and end. Sit by the small fountain under the canopy of old trees and just relax. There's a small cafeteria, vending machines and bathrooms nearby too.

8. Climb The Ottoman Cannons

Across the road from the visitor's center, you'll see another piece of the Old Wall. This one has real cannons too! Kids love climbing on these authentic cannons that date back to Napoleon's time. These metal weapons actually saved Akko from being taken over by the French emperor!

9. See A Museum

Akko has several art museums and galleries that are well worth a visit. If you want to stick to the historic perspective, the Treasures In The Wall museum is your best bet. These rich collections of crafts and objects from various periods are on display literally within the old wall (hence the name of this museum).

10. Enjoy The Akko Festival

Yes, I know, this post is supposed to offer you nine awesome things to do in Akko. Here's a bonus tenth item! This one is very seasonal, so maybe it should be numbered "nine and a half"?

Getting to the point, Akko is home to the Israeli Festival of Fringe Theatre. Every year during the Jewish holiday of Sukkot, the city turns into a local Edinburgh. The shows themselves are usually in Hebrew but there are many street performances outside too. The exact dates change each year according to the Jewish holiday calendar but if you're planning on visiting Israel during September or October find out if you can catch this very special festival

Suggested Itinerary For One Day In Akko

Here's a textual description of your day in Akko. I'm going to assume arrival at around 9AM. If you think that's too early, I would suggest arriving the day before and spending the night there. Of you could just start your day later and adjust the itinerary accordingly.

9 AM Arrive at the Visitor Center (there's parking nearby if you're coming with a car). Get a map and buy your ticket for visiting the various locations. They offer a discounted rate

if you buy everything in advance. There's a short introductory film at the Visitors Center that's worth watching. You can get a coffee while waiting for the film to start and sip it next the old fountain.

10 AM-Noon Visit the Halls and the Medieval market (plenty to see there)

Noon-1 PM Visit the Hammam and watch the show there

1 PM-3 PM Stroll in the market streets. This is a great time to grab lunch and I marked Hummus Said for you in the map if that's what you feel like eating. Plenty of other places to buy snacks, falafel or sit down for lunch.

3 PM Enter the Templar Tunnel from the market entrance. It's open until 6:30 so you have plenty of time (just note that if you didn't

get your ticket in advance, you can get your ticket here until 5:30. Follow in the footsteps of the knights and cross the tunnel to the other side. You'll emerge right in front of the beautiful blue mediterranean sea.

3:30-4:30 Stroll along the walls. As you leave the tunnel, turn left and you'll see the steps that take you up the walls. Walk on the wall for fantastic views of the sea and city.

17:00 Visit the cannons. From the walls, you can choose to walk through the market area again, or just outside it (plenty of stalls everywhere, don't worry), to the old cannons on the hill.

If you happened to be super fast, you may get to the cannons at around 4 PM, leaving you with just enough time to visit the nearby

Treasures in the Walls Museum which closes at 5.

You're not back where you started. If you've had enough, you can start heading back. Otherwise, keep exploring and enjoy the Old City of Akko at night. I would suggest an early dinner in one of the restaurants overlooking the sea for a great sunset!

There's a lot to see and do in Akko and even more around it. If you have any questions I'd love to try and help leave me a comment here. Or just let me know what you think of Akko if you would like to visit someday or have visited and have your own tips to share!

Best Things to Do in Acre Akko [Israel Off the Beaten Path]

Standing at the top of Akko's eastern walls, we take a deep breath of the salty air and let the Israeli sun warm our backs. Fall is the perfect time to visit Israel and we could not have chosen a better day to discover Akko's hidden gems. From up here, we can see Akko's port and the mishmash of houses and streets, colorful clothes blowing in the wind on the washing lines, the blues and greens of the mosques what a beautiful mess!

This ancient port city in the north of Israel has many names. Most tourists know it as Acre, in Arabic it is known as Akka but the locals call it Akko. Akko's history dates back to the bronze age and many of the world's most influential leaders have passed through old Acre at some point or another, from England's King Richard I and France's King Philipp II to Napoleon who tried to conquer Acre in 1799 but did not succeed.

Akko is one of the most fascinating cities in Israel not only because of its rich history but also because of the mixture of cultures and the sense of community. Officially about 70% of Akko's residents are Jews while the other 30% are Arabs but inside the Old City the majority are Muslim Arabs, there are some Christian Arabs and very few Jews. There are so many things to do and see in and around Akko so it's such a shame that many tourists don't put it on their Israel bucket list since it's a great destination to discover Israel off the beaten path. You can find in Akko's Old City so many attractions for anyone who loves history, art, authenticity, photography, great food and more. From colorful markets, ancient fortresses, art museums, attractions for children, great restaurants, sunny beaches and more Akko will not disappoint you, it will probably be amongst the highlights of your Israel itinerary.

Reasons to Put Akko on Your Off the Beaten Path Israel Itinerary

- Only 1.5 hours by car from Tel Aviv (there's also a train that takes a bit longer)
- The Old City of Akko was declared as a UNESCO World Heritage Site.
- To escape the crowds of Tel Aviv and Jerusalem and discover Israel off the beaten path.
- A variety of attractions located in close proximity

- To have a taste of the more authentic side of Israel.

- Akko can be a great base from which you can take day trips all over the north of Israel, to Haifa, Rosh Hanikra, the Galilee and the Golan Heights.

Akko's location and natural harbor have attracted many people over the years from the Crusaders to Ottoman rulers, everyone wanted to take advantage of its strategic location. Many treasures from the East that are now common ingredients in every household, passed through Acre's harbor to Europe, cones of sugar, exotic spices and even pasta. Wandering around the maze of narrow streets, you'll find remnants from different eras, some are open for tourists while others are being restored. Some of Akko's historic treasures were built on top of each other, so, on the one hand, there is this underground city from around the crusaders time and above the ground, you can find the remnants of the Ottoman rulers. Here are some of the things to do in Akko to learn more about its history and discover Israel off the beaten path.

One of the best things to do in Akko is to visit the Knights kingdom. This must-see attraction is a large compound where you can learn about the crusaders who used to live in old Acre. Start by watching the explanatory movie at the visitor center (very kid friendly), rest for a while in the beautiful garden (the Enchanted Garden) and then start exploring the Hospitaller Fortress and Knights Halls.

Hospitaller Fortress and Knights Hall

The Hospitaller Order was a military-monastic order that treated the sick in the Holy Land. They arrived at Acre in the 12th century and stayed there till the end of the 13th century. Visiting the Hospitaller Fortress is a great experience for the whole family. These halls had been covered by sand and dirt by the Ottoman rulers who built their own fortress on top of them. Nowadays, after the restoration work, strolling through the different halls, it is easy to imagine the hundreds of knights who lived here so many years ago. Don't forget to visit the old dining hall (Hall of Columns) which is the most impressive part of the complex. In the Pillars Hall you can visit the art and craft market where you can buy natural soap, handcrafted glass, and other unique souvenirs. The admission fee includes an electronic tour guide to help you uncover the history and stories of the Hospitaller Fortress. Strolling around this compound is one of the best things to do in Akko, so make sure to visit it.

Pro Tip: From July till September (and during Jewish holidays such as Passover or Sukkot), you can watch the re-enactment of tournaments of knights every Saturday. It's a great attraction for families with kids. For more details about the Knights' Tournament.

Templars Tunnel

The Templars were a military-monastic order that helped pilgrims who came to visit the Holy Land. The Templars Fortress was located near the shore and today you might catch a glimpse of it under the water near Akko's lighthouse. Akko's Templars Tunnel was built to enable the

Templars to move commodities and money from Acre's port to their fortress. Nowadays you can walk through it from side to side.

Visit Akko's Markets

Local markets are always at the top of our things to do in every destination and even if you've already been to Jerusalem's and Tel Aviv's markets, Akko's market has its own distinction. Stroll among the stands, taste some of the best street food and sweets in Israel and learn about the ingredients of the Israeli cuisine. Akko's market is a great place to buy spices, coffee and unique delicacies and there is plenty of fresh fish and seafood as well. Another local initiative is the Turkish Bazaar. Originally, it was built in the late 18th century as a municipal market to provide services for Acre's residents and in recent years it has been renovated and reopened as an art and craft bazaar. There are a few good eateries here as well as some small souvenirs shops.

Take a Walk on Acre's Walls

Akko's walls are famous all over the world. The old walls of Acre have protected it from numerous armies throughout history. The original walls were first built in 950 by Ibn Tolon and since then they have been renovated multiple times by different rulers. The walls themselves might not be very high or long but they are quite wide and inside these walls there used to be horse stables and torture chambers. Nowadays you can see the cannons on the eastern walls (that protected the land), and more importantly, it is a great viewpoint (just climb carefully to the highest part). You can also visit the Treasures in the Walls

Museum that has been built inside some of the original halls that used to belong to the Ottoman soldiers. The western walls start from the lighthouse and are referred to as the sea walls. Walking on the western walls from the lighthouse inward you'll see Akko from a different point of view. You'll get a different viewpoint of the Mediterranean Sea, but you'll also get a glimpse into the inner neighborhoods of Akko. If you're lucky you'll get to see the local teens dive into the water from the top of the walls.

Akko's old port has its own charm. In the early morning you can meet the fishermen who come back from the sea and later in the day, just stroll around and soak in the vibes and sea breeze or hop on a boat tour to see Akko's walls from a different perspective. You can also take a pick at Akko's Khan al-Umdan and its clock tower. The building is one of the most impressive ones in Akko but unfortunately, it's currently closed (recently it has been announced that a luxury hotel is going to be built there). Taking great pictures is also high up on our list of things to do and if you walk almost to the end of the marina, you'll find the perfect Instagram spot to take pictures of the marina with the backdrop of Akko.

Get Lost in Akko's Cobbled Stone Streets and Discover Akko's Hidden Gems

Wandering around aimlessly in narrow cobbled stone streets with our cameras in our hands is our favorite way to spend the day. If we happen to stumble upon tiny bakeries, colorful street art, local kids playing in back alleys, a small shop of a seamstress or the studio of the local stone sculptor and other such sights, well, we can tick off a couple of other highlights from our favorite things to do list. Akko's Old City is a UNESCO World Heritage Site but it is also a living breathing city where you'll witness the everyday lives of the residents. It is a place to capture unique photographs, an opportunity to discover where the locals buy their freshly baked Za'atar covered pita that is baked in the oldest oven in Akko, a maze where you'll find simple local residential houses near a high-end boutique hotel and so much more. It is very small so it's not that easy to get lost but if you do, just ask the friendly locals who'll gladly help you.

Visit Akko's Museums

There are a couple of very unique and interesting museums in Akko such as the

Okashi Art Museum. The building dates back to the Ottoman period and inside you'll find rotating exhibitions of local artists as well as a permanent exhibition of Avshalom Okashi's work. Okashi was one of Israel's most famous artists and spent most of his life in Akko. We have already mentioned the Treasures in the Walls Museum which is built inside the halls of the eastern walls. This museum holds collections that showcase the life of the Galilee residents in the 19th 20th centuries. Another interesting museum is The Underground Prisoners Museum which is located in the Citadel of Akko. For more information about Acre's museums.

Experience a Real Hammam at Ghattas Turkish Bath

There's no better time than a vacation to spoil yourself with a spa treatment or a massage or better yet, a traditional Turkish bath. Ghattas Turkish Bath includes a hammam, a steam room, dry sauna, jacuzzi and massage treatments. Emil Ghattas was born and raised in Akko's Old City and after finding success in the High-Tech field, he decided to come back home and fulfill an old childhood dream. While he was growing up in the 1950s, the local hammams were very popular since many of the households did not have running water or bathtubs. Once the majority of the houses had a regular supply of water and electricity, the traditional hammams were abandoned. Finally, after years of visiting hammams in other countries, Emil decided to buy an old building (from the Ottoman period) in Akko's Old City, renovate it and turn it into a luxury bathhouse. There are several treatments to choose from but the traditional and most popular ones are the scrub treatment and the Turkish massage. Once you make a reservation, you'll get the Turkish bath area just for yourself (for two hours), without any other guests around. For more details and the variety of treatments check Ghattas Turkish Bath.

Top Restaurants in Akko, Israel

Akko (Acre) is situated on Israel's northern Mediterranean coastline and is home to an ancient and enchanting Old City. Declared a UNESCO World Heritage Site in 2001, its extraordinarily well-preserved Crusader walls surround its vibrant Arab *shuk,* charming cobbled streets and fascinating historical sites that have witnessed Byzantine, Crusader, Islamic and Ottoman rule. It is also a foodie's paradise, with an array of fabulous restaurants, from hummus joints to gourmet seafood. Here are our top picks.

Uri Buri
Restaurant, Seafood
Uri Buri is widely considered one of the finest fish restaurants in Israel. Located a stone's throw from the sea inside an unpretentious Ottoman-era building, it serves fresh fish and creative seafood dishes along with over 100 different kinds of fine Israeli wine. Head chef, Uri Jeremias, is a legendary figure in Israel's culinary scene and his food is an absolute must for any trip to Akko.

Ha-Hagana Street, Acre, North District, Israel.
+97249552212

Hummus Said
Restaurant, Market, Israeli, Middle Eastern
This Akko institution has been serving up delicious hummus for generations. Located in the heart of the Old City's vibrant Arab shuk, the smooth, creamy consistency of their handmade hummus and will leave your stomach and soul feeling nourished. Regarded by many Israelis as the best hummus spot in the country (quite a feat), Hummus Said is worth a trip to Akko on its own. To beat the lines and to eat in a slightly quieter atmosphere, come early.
Acre, North District, Israel. +97249913945

Doniana
Restaurant, Israeli, Middle Eastern, Mediterranean
Dreamy views meet delicious seafood and meat at this Akko restaurant. Perched over the Mediterranean Sea, facing the ancient walls of Akko's Old City, Doniana's menu features fresh

grilled fish and tender meats accompanied by a plethora of side dishes. This is probably the most scenic dining spot in the city and it's perfect for a romantic date.

+97249910001

Mercato
Restaurant, Italian, Middle Eastern
Located in Akko's picturesque Turkish Bazaar, Mercato is an intimate and highly rated spot serving up delicious Italian dishes with a touch of the Middle East. From authentic Neapolitan pizza made in their wood oven to fresh calamari and handmade pasta full of scrumptious flavours, this enchanting restaurant is an Akko gem.

El Marsa
Restaurant, Middle Eastern, Mediterranean
El Marsa is located on Akko's port and is a must for seafood lovers. They serve the freshest fish,

from calamari rings and shrimp to fillet of lavrak (a local white fish) and salmon, in addition to meats and interesting desserts, such as halva mousse. Aside from the delicious food, the restaurant itself is situated in a converted 13th century home that makes this a particularly special dining atmosphere. Oh, and it overlooks the glistening Mediterranean Sea.

Talmi Street, Acre, North District, Israel.+97249019281

Quick Guide for New Travelers

Akko(עכו), also known as 'Akka(عكّا) and to Westerners as Acre, lies on the northern edge of the Bay of Acre in northern Israel. On its present site, Akko possesses a long history of various cultures: Canaanites, Phoenicians, Greeks, Romans, Crusaders and Arabs. Akko is a holy city in the Bahá'í Faith and in spite of its small size has two UNESCO World Heritage Sites: (1) the Old City of Acre; and (2) the Baha'i garden of Acre, which is a part of the Baha'i Holy Places in Haifa and the Western Galilee.

Understand

If you found Jerusalem too intense, come to Acre to find a magnificent coastal Old City with a slower pace. There's plenty to see (and hear and taste and smell!) above ground and below. If you're okay with crowds, Acre can make a great place to spend a Saturday, as the Old City doesn't close down and the attractions are open. It's possible to see Acre as a day-trip from Haifa, but to get the full experience, plan to stay a night. If you're looking to take a few days to relax on your trip, Acre makes a great place to slow down for a few days and enjoy the Old City and beaches.

Acre's Old City is populated mainly by Palestinian citizens of Israel (Muslim and Christian), and the New City is mainly Jewish-Israeli. The neighborhoods immediately outside the Old City are mixed. The city as a whole boasts a highly diverse population, and in addition to Arabic and Hebrew, you may hear Russian, Azerbaijani, and Ukrainian spoken on the streets by city residents.

Get in
Getting to Akko (Acre) is very simple, as it lays on the north of Haifa and on the main Israeli train track.

By train
Israel Railways. Every 20 minutes in peak hours. 35.50 from Tel Aviv, 13.50 from Haifa. Israel

Railways, Israel's only train operator, has over 40 daily trains to and from Akko every 20 minutes during peak hours. Most of these trains go all the way to Tel Aviv and Ben Gurion Airport.

By bus
Egged. 11.70 from Haifa and from Carmiel. Israel's national bus company, has a slighty slower and cheaper connection to Akko, with bus lines 271, 272 and 251. Lines 361, 262 and 500 connect Akko with Carmiel.

NTT. 21.50 from Nazareth. Line 353, operating about once an hour Sunday to Friday morning, speeds you from Nazareth to Acre (or the reverse) in under an hour. Drops you just outside of the Old City. Get off at the Marine Officers School (Beit Sefer L'Katzinei Yam) or if you miss it, Ha'Arba'a Road (Derech H'Arba'a).

By taxi

Service taxis travel frequently from the Hadar neighborhood of Haifa to Akko. They are as cheap or cheaper than the bus. Look for a sign saying "Akko Naharia" or "Akko Karmiel" in Hebrew only in the front of the service taxi. If you don't know Hebrew, go to Herzl street in Haifa, point an index finger at a 45 degree angle with the ground (the Israeli hitchhiking signal) when a service taxi drives by, and ask where it's going.

By road

Parking in the Old City has become a serious problem on Fridays and Saturdays. If you are staying the night on one of these days, call your accommodation ahead of time to confirm that you need a parking place and they should help to guide you to a suitable location.

Get around

The Old City is small and basically pedestrian only. It is a 10 minute walk from the bus station and 15-20 minute walk from the train station. NTT bus 353 to Nazareth drops off on the road into town, a 5 minute walk from the Old City, and the longer Egged bus 343 from Nazareth drops off in the Old City.

The only major site outside the Old City is the Bahá'í shrine. You can take a private cab there, or else a "sherut" taxi going north to Nahariya can drop you off on the road outside the shrine.

From the Old City, walk out to Ben Ami St a couple of blocks into the New City and follow it all the way to Tel Akko (or Tel Napoleon), a Bronze Age-Hellenistic period archaeological site. It is free to visit and worth it if you are looking for some peace and quiet. The site is currently being excavated, so there is little signage, but it has incredible views over the bay, to the south, and the hills of the Lebanon border, to the north.

See
- The wall has a lot of history to offer, and you can walk atop a section dating from the rule of Ahmed Al-Jazzar from the breach at Weizman St to the Land Gate at the sea shore. The wall also houses the Treasures in the Wall Ethnographic Museum. It is fun to walk along, especially the part bordering the sea. In 1750, Daher El-Omar, the ruler of Acre, utilized the remnants of the Crusader walls as a foundation for his walls. Two gates were set in the wall, the "land gate" in the eastern wall, and the "sea gate" in the

southern wall. In 1912 the Acre lighthouse was built on the south-western corner of the walls.

- Hall of the Crusader Knights at the Citadel. Under the citadel and prison of Acre, archaeological excavations revealed a complex of halls built and used by the Hospitallers Knights. This complex was a part of the Hospitallers' citadel in the northern area of medieval Acre. The complex includes six semi-joined halls, one recently excavated large hall, a dungeon, a dining room and the crypt of an ancient Gothic church. Some of the buildings and houses around (and including) St. Andrew's Church and the Pisan port have Crusader-era foundations, and most of the roads and squares in the city follow the same layout as the Crusader city. There were also residential quarters and marketplaces run by merchants from Pisa and Amalfi in Crusader and medieval Acre.

- The Templar Tunnel was built by the Knights Templar to provide underground passage between their fortress, which stood near the current lighthouse, to the port on the south-eastern side of the city. The tunnel was recently excavated and access is included on the combined ticket.

- The synagogue of the Ramchal (Rabbi Moshe Chaim Luzzatto) a Kabbalah master. Look for it on the map available for 3 NIS at the ticket office. Knock on the door and there is a friendly interpreter who is usually there during the day to show you around.

- Hammam al-Basha Built in 1795 by Jezzar Pasha, Acre's hammam has a series of hot rooms and a hexagonal steam room with a marble fountain. It was used by the Irgun as a bridge to break into the citadel's prison. The bathhouse kept functioning until 1950. Now it is a tourist site featuring an entertaining video presentation of Acre's past (as told by the hammam's last operator and his ancestors).

- The citadel of Acre and Underground Prisoners Museum is an Ottoman fortification, built on the foundation of the Hospitaller citadel. The citadel was part of the city's defensive formation, reinforcing the northern wall. During the 20th century the citadel was used mainly as a prison and as the site for a gallows. During the British mandate period, activists of Jewish Zionist resistance movements were held prisoner there; several were executed there. The Irgun staged a famous prison break against the citadel in May 1947, which is commemorated by a monument nearby. Famous characters like Baha'u'llah and Israel's prime minister Menachem Begin used to be locked there. Today the site is managed by the Ministry of Defense, so bring your passport if you plan to visit.

- Or Torah, Tunisian synagogue, a meticulously handcrafted spectacle of stained glass and tile mosaic entirely unique to Akko. (located a 3-5 minute walk outside the Old City from the Land Gate)

- Khan el Umdan Old Akko has several large khans (an inn enclosing a courtyard, used by caravans for accommodation) which once served the camel caravans bringing in grain from the hinterland. The grandest is the Khan al-Umdan . Its name means 'Inn of the Pillars', and it was built by Al-Jazzar in 1785. The pillars that give the khan its name were looted from Caesarea. It is a two story structure and the ground floor would have housed the animals, while their merchant owners would have slept upstairs. It is currently part of a real estate dispute and thus usually closed. Peak through the gate from the entrance on Venice (or Fishermen's) Square.

- Okashi Art Museum Around the corner from the Hamman al-Basha is a gallery devoted to the works of Avshalom Okashi (1916-80), an influential Israeli painter and a resident of Akko for the last half of his life. Included in the combined ticket (with Crusader Halls, Templar Tunnel, Treasures in the Wall).

- The Great Mosque of Jezzar Pasha was built in 1781. Jezzar Pasha and his successor Suleiman Pasha, are both buried in a small graveyard adjacent to the mosque. In a shrine on the second level of the mosque, a single hair from the prophet Mohammed's beard is kept and shown on special ceremonial occasions.

- The Pisan Port now occupied by three restaurants on the southern end of the Old City. Impressive Crusader masonry can still be seen.

- The Shrine of Baha'u'llah the holiest place for the Bahá'ís. The Shrine of Bahá'u'lláh is composed of a central room that has a small garden at its centre, which has trees growing in it and there are layers of carpets around the walls. In the right hand corner of the central room there is a small room where Bahá'u'lláh's remains are laid to rest.

- The Market mostly local shops with a few oriented toward travelers. A good place to buy spices, olive oil soaps, loofas, coffee, and tea.

- Tel Akko the remains of the ancient city of Acre before it was resettled on the piece of land currently known as the "Old City" in the Hellenistic period with incredible views of the Old City, Haifa, villages to east, and the sea. Take a walk down Ben-Ami Street, past the shopping mall about 15 minutes from the Old City. You'll find a massive hill with a statue of Napoleon Bonaparte on top. The hill, or "tel", results from multiple ancient cities built on top of each other from the Early Bronze Age to the Hellenistic Period (i.e. Canaanites to Alexander the Great). In antiquity, the site was an important trading port with goods being traded between the Levant, the Aegean, Anatolia, Cyprus, and Egypt. Excavations are ongoing, and you might catch some archaeologists if you visit in July. Free, and since few travelers know about it, is well worth a visit if you're craving some peace and quiet.

- The Turkish Bazaar The newly renovated bazaar in the old city, where several up-and-coming chefs have opened small restaurants. A couple of good souvenir shops with products made in-country too.

- Tomb of Sheikh Izz al-Din This maqam (shrine) is located on the beach approximately 1.5km north of the old city of Akko. This is a square (4.5m per side) domed building standing in an area of open scrub. The entrance to the tomb is on the south side and is protected with an iron door. There is a window on the west side from which it is possible to see that the floor level inside is considerably (0.5m) lower than the outside ground level.

- Tomb of al-Khader is a Druze shrine in the village of Kafr Yassif near Akko this is the tomb of St.George (on its Muslim/Druze verison and name) according to the Druze faith.

- Tomb of Sheikh Amin Tarif The tomb of Sheikh Amin Tarif is located in the village of Julis near Acre. Sheikh Amin Tarif was the leader of the Druze community during the British Mandate of Palestine and the State of Israel periods. he was also known for all the Druze worldwide religious activity. he was died in 1993 and buried in his home in Julis. today his home is also a Maqam (Shrine) and many Druze pilgrims visiting his tomb.

Do
- Join the crowd and smoke nargileh (or just have a tea) in the recently restored Khan esh-Shwarda in the evening.
- Do the rounds at all the hummus restaurants of the old city it might take a couple days, but it's the best around.

- Visit the Turkish Bazaar. On some Saturday afternoons there are lively performances and visiting artisans.

- Take a boat ride around the walls of the old city.

- Watch the kids jumping off the eastern wall into the Mediterranean Sea.

- Get scrubbed down at Hammam Ghattas (advance reservations required)

Learn
- AlMadrasa is a school and workshop offering short (1.5 hours) and long courses (up to multiple weeks) in traditional stone carving and stone sculpting. Caters to school groups, professionals, and visitors to the city. (advance notice suggested)

Buy

You can buy almost anything along the main marketplace ask and someone will direct you! Sea sponges, olive oil soaps, spices, tobacco and pipes, perfumes can all be found, usually cheaper than in Jerusalem. Be aware, though, that unless you have excellent haggling skills in Arabic or Hebrew, you will still be paying marked up prices. Settle on your price before you agree to make a purchase to avoid an awkward situation.

Eat
You can find delicious hummus throughout Acre, and baklava or knafeh in the old bazaar.

Acre is famous for its fish restaurants, some of the best are located in the port area. Doniana and Abu Christo are classics, a must for anyone who wants to have a great meal in a great location looking over the sea.

Eat everywhere. On Salah ah-Din Street there are bakeries with yummy treats. Foods like this are hard to find. Rough it up and enjoy the experience.

If you are looking for quality upscale dining, options include Uri Buri, located on the lagoon walkway on HaHagana Street, and El Marsa, located at the the marina.

There are some newer, small, and terrific restaurants in the Turkish Bazaar if you come out of the Crusader Halls feeling hungry.

A little far away from the crowds of the old city is the locals favorite Gallery Simaan restaurant, located at Ben Ami street (no. 63)

Drink
Marsa Bar, tucked into a back room of El Marsa restaurant at the marina, is the only real bar in

the Old City, but it's a good one. Beer on tap and an extensive cocktail menu. It's also possible to order food from the restaurant.

Bader Coffee in the main market sells coffee from around the world. Ask him to grind it with cardamom to get the local flavor. He also brews a good espresso for 5 NIS.

Hummus El-Abed Abu Hmid (under the lighthouse) in addition to delicious plates of hummus or ful or daily specials you'd normally only find in local kitchens, is a great place to stop for coffee or tea.

Alcohol is served at most of the larger Old City restaurants; most will be happy to serve beer or arak without food. Nothing quite compares to having a few drinks at Abu Christo by the marina at sunset.

Sleep

- Akkommodation (Hotel Akkommodation in Akko), Saleh el-Basri St. (Enter the Old City from the coast, you see the lighthouse, continue to the left on Saleh el-Basri Street), +972-544-496-525. checkin: 3:00; checkout: 12:00. A refurbished boutique hotel at the coast of the old city of Akko with a breathtaking view on the Mediterranean sea. Along the eastern wall of Akko in a picturesque narrow lane across two outstanding restaurants. Uniquely designed rooms with kitchen and private bathroom and eager-to-please innkeepers make it a affordable option in Akko. 135 per night.

- Walid's Gate Hostel which may also be seen as the "Akko Gate Hostel" is dodgy indeed (not asking to see passport, no keys for rooms), but the experience is worthwhile, and very affordable. Backpackers roughing it up will enjoy a roof over their heads for such a low price. Accommodation is provided in a large dorm room with bunk and normal beds. Price is 90 per person per night.

- The Acco Guest House of Zippi in Bilu street, is a warm, family-owned, budget hostel, situated in a walking distance from the Old City of Akko. Suitable for a short vacation or for a long stay for independent travelers, backpackers and families traveling in Akko, Safed and the Galilee.

- Akkotel, Salahudin St. (Enter Old City on Weizman, continue to the left on Salah ad Din), +972-4-9877100. checkin: 3:00;

checkout: 12:00. A refurbished boutique hotel along the eastern wall of the old city. Uniquely designed rooms with high ceilings and hand made furniture, and eager-to-please innkeepers make it a great upscale option in Akko. 600 per night.

- Rimonim Palm Beach Hotel Acre, Seashore, P.O.Box 2192, Acre (Located on the beach close to the town. Akko station is about 1km from the hotel.), +972-4-9877777. checkin: 3 PM; checkout: 11 AM. Hotel situated on the coastal stretch of Israel. The Rimonim Palm Beach Hotel is a unique combination of 127 modern rooms and suites with a health and sports club, a spa and superb conference facilities. The panoramic views of Haifa Bay and Akko are spectacular

- Nzar Khoury for Hosting, Old City 11/83, Acre (Walking toward the lighthouse on Ha-Hagana St, look for a house with a dozen or so statues in front. Head up the stairs next to it, and turn left at the top. Look up and you'll see the sign.), +972-544-622-428. checkin: 12:00; checkout: 11:00. Rooms are basic but comfortable, all with en-suite bathrooms. Spectacular sunset views over the lighthouse and the sea. 250 per night.

- Sand Hostel, Haim Weizman 1, Acre. That is the closest address there is, in the small streets there are no names. (At the corner of Salah Ad-din street and Haim Weizman Street there is a entrance going towards the Turkish Bazaar going West. After passing the Bazaar on your right the path will split, turn right, there is a sign. Follow the signs and you'll see a green door on your right, walk through and you've made it), (+972)050-908-3402 (akko.sand.hostel@gmail.com). checkin: 12:00; checkout: 11:00. Rooms are beautifully designed with a TV, air-conditioning and storage. All bed rooms have their own bathrooms, while dormitories share a bathroom. Bathrooms are clean and rooms have a special old city atmosphere. 80 per night in dorms, 250 double, available for family with 100 extra for each extra person in the room..

Get out

NTT bus line 353 makes access to Nazareth quick and easy for a day trip. From Nazareth there are easy connections to Haifa, and it is also possible to access the West Bank via a 25 minute taxi to the Jalame checkpoint.

Haifa is also easily accessible for day trips either by bus or train. On Saturday, Haifa is also accessible by sherut (shared taxi) from Derech Ha'Arba'a in the New City

The End